Montana State Capitol

Helena

Jane Moorman

There is a saying, "It was a Friday night and it seemed like a good idea at the time." That sums up the beginning of the State Capitols Project.

When photographer Jane Moorman told her brother of her idea of photographing state capitols, he said, "You do know there are 50 states and two of them you can't drive to."

Her answer was, "Your point is? It gives me a good reason to visit every state."

Montana: Big Sky Country

Under the broad blue skies that give the state one of its nicknames, Big Sky Country Montana's state capitol was built in two phases.

The first phase of the American Renaissance design building, the rotunda section with two wings, was designed by architects Charles E. Bell and John H. Kent. Work began in 1899 and was completed in 1902.

Within 10 years, the second phase that expanded the legislative wings was completed. These additions were designed by architects Frank Mills Andrews, Charles S. Haire and John C. Link.

The first section's exterior material was Columbus sandstone, with Montana granite used in the second section.

During the construction, the arrival of the 17-foot-tall statue that tops the capitol's dome was a surprise to the builders. It arrived at the train station with only a label identifying the shipper as a foundry in the east. There was no record of who ordered it or where it was to be placed.

Part of the problem was that the former capitol commission had absconded with most of the records when the commission was disbanded because of its plans to scam money from the building project.

Adding to the mystery, the foundry records from where the statue was ordered were destroyed in a fire.

Without any information as to where the statue was intended, a decision was made to place it atop the dome and name it Lady Liberty.

In 2006, a Pennsylvania woman contacted the Montana Historical Society inquiring if her grandfather's statue was still atop the dome.

Historians were able to confirm that the woman's claim was true. It was learned that the Belgian-born sculptor, Edward J. Van Landeghem, had named the statue "Montana."

The walls and ceilings throughout the capitol are decorated with paintings depicting Montana's history.

Of those, the House of Representatives chamber is home to a masterpiece painting by the nationally acclaimed artist, Charles M. Russell. The painting 25-feet-long and 12-feet-high depicts Lewis and Clark meeting Montana's Bitterroot Salish people.

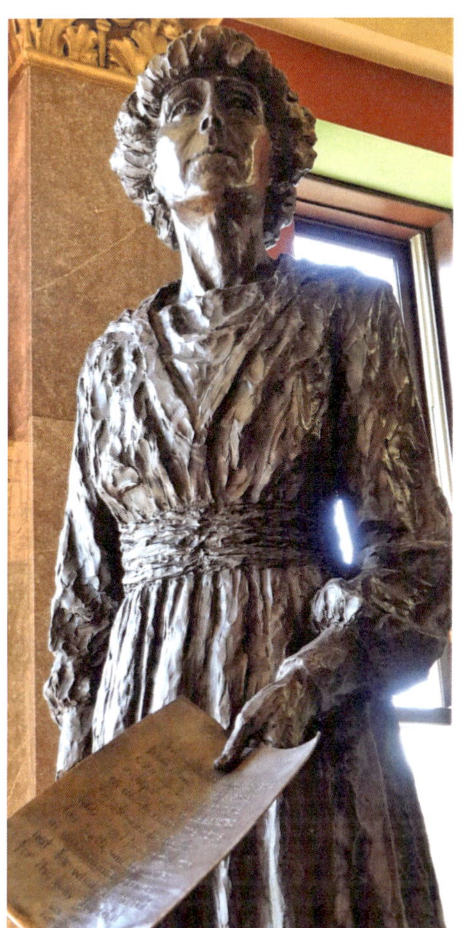

Jeannette Rankins

Jeannette Rankins is honored by a bronze statue created by Terry Mimanaugh in 1980.

Rankin was a leading suffragist and peace advocate. She was the first woman democratically elected to the U.S. Congress in 1916 and the only person to vote against the U.S.'s entry into both World Wars I and II.

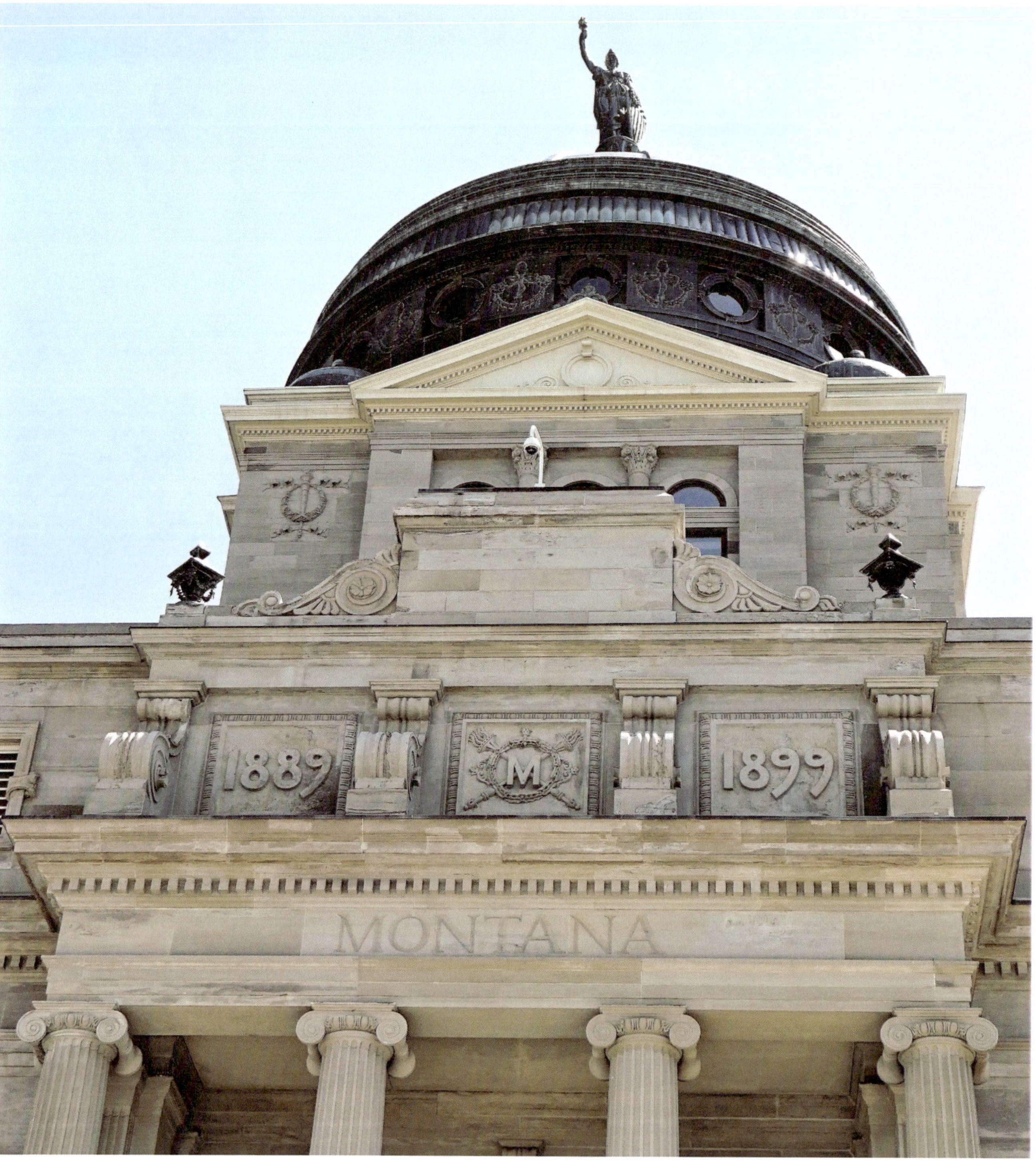

1889
M
1899
MONTANA

'Montana' reigns over Copper Dome

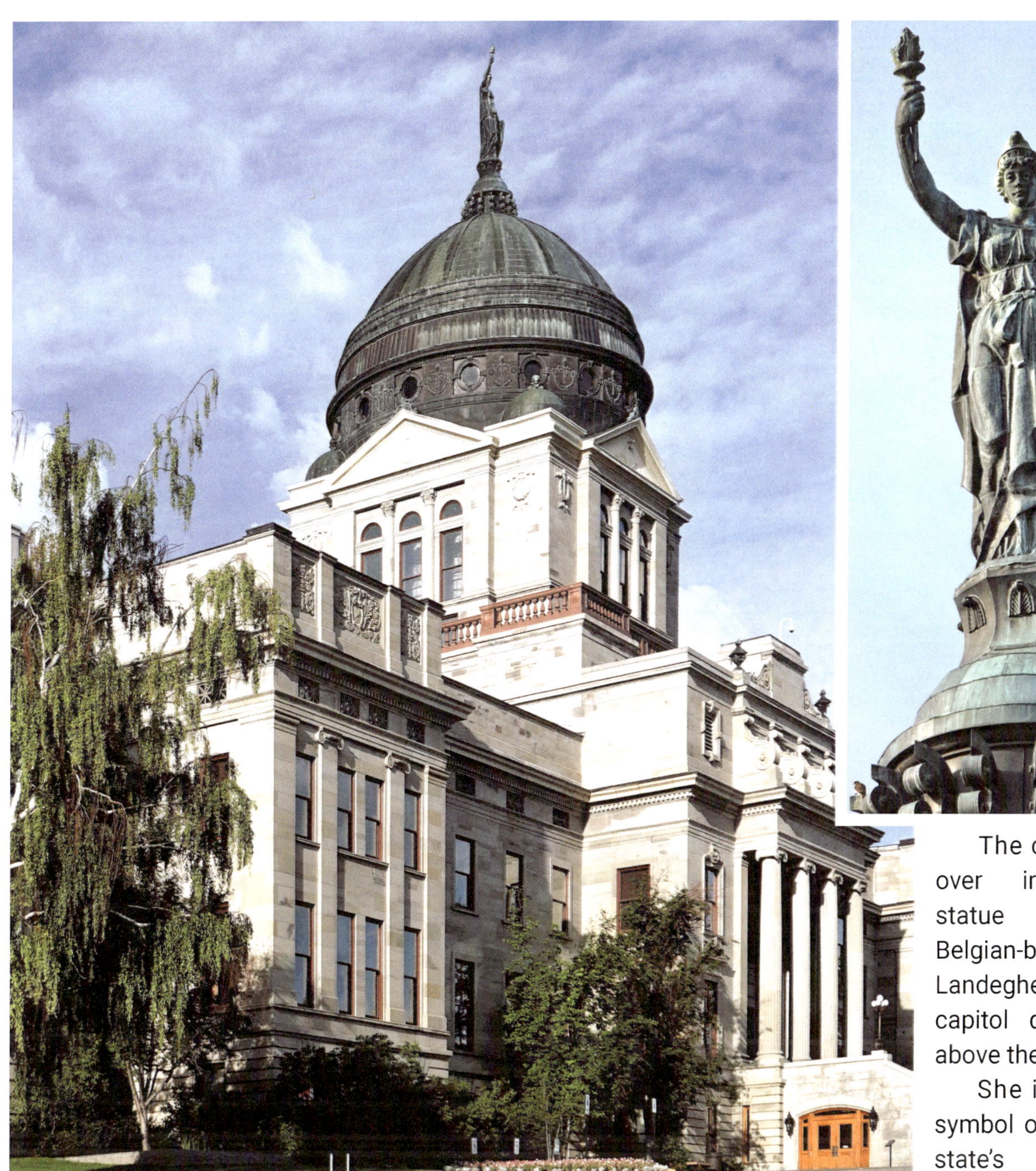

The copper sheeting over iron framework statue Montana, by Belgian-born Edward Van Landeghem, graces the capitol dome, 165 feet above the ground.

She is the classical symbol of liberty and the state's dedication to democracy.

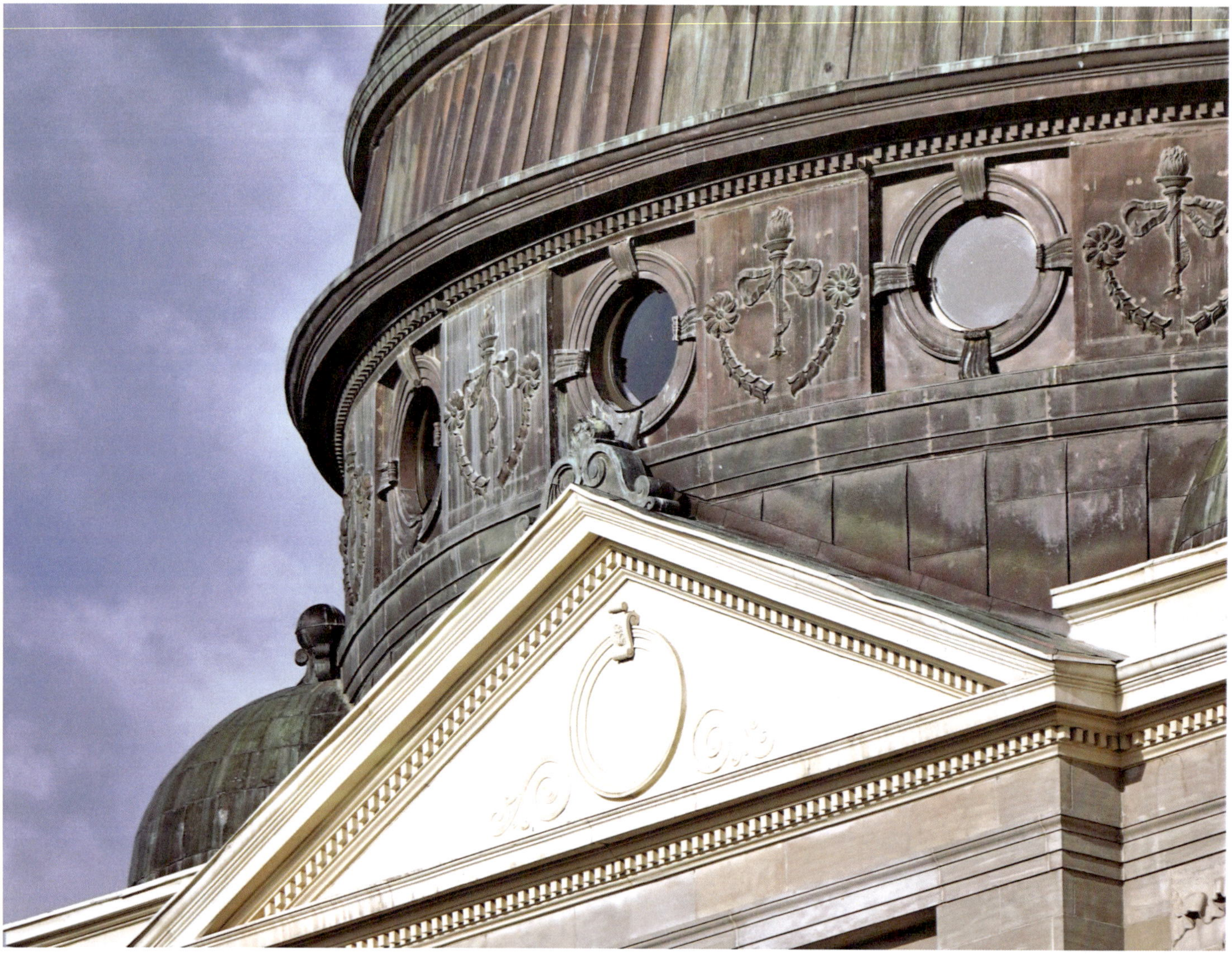

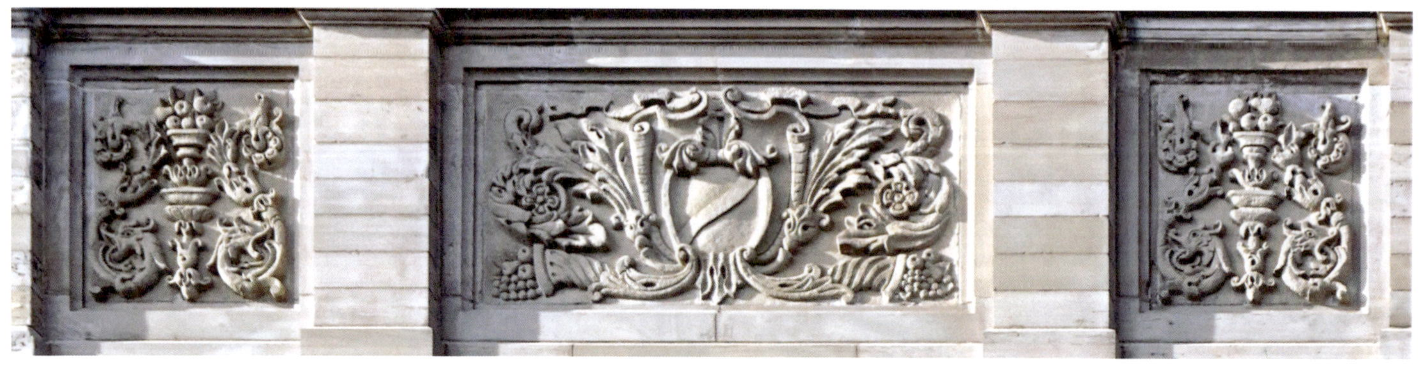

Thomas Francis Meagher 'Meagher of the Sword' Equestrian Statue

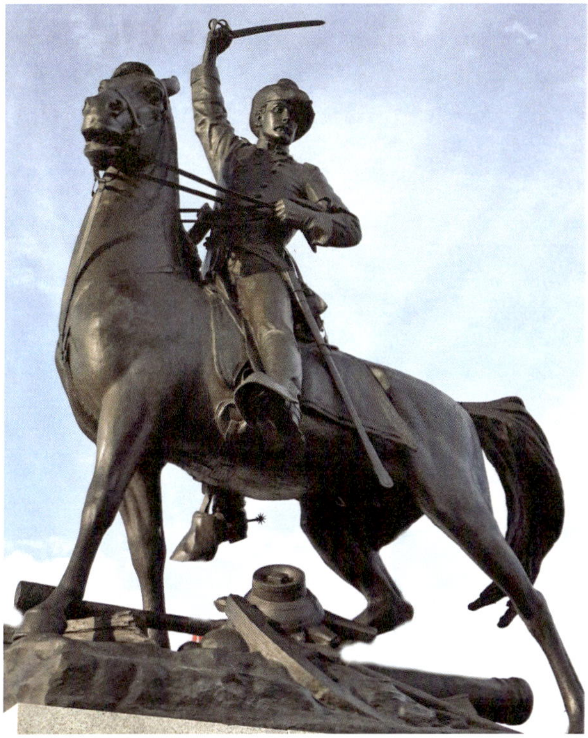

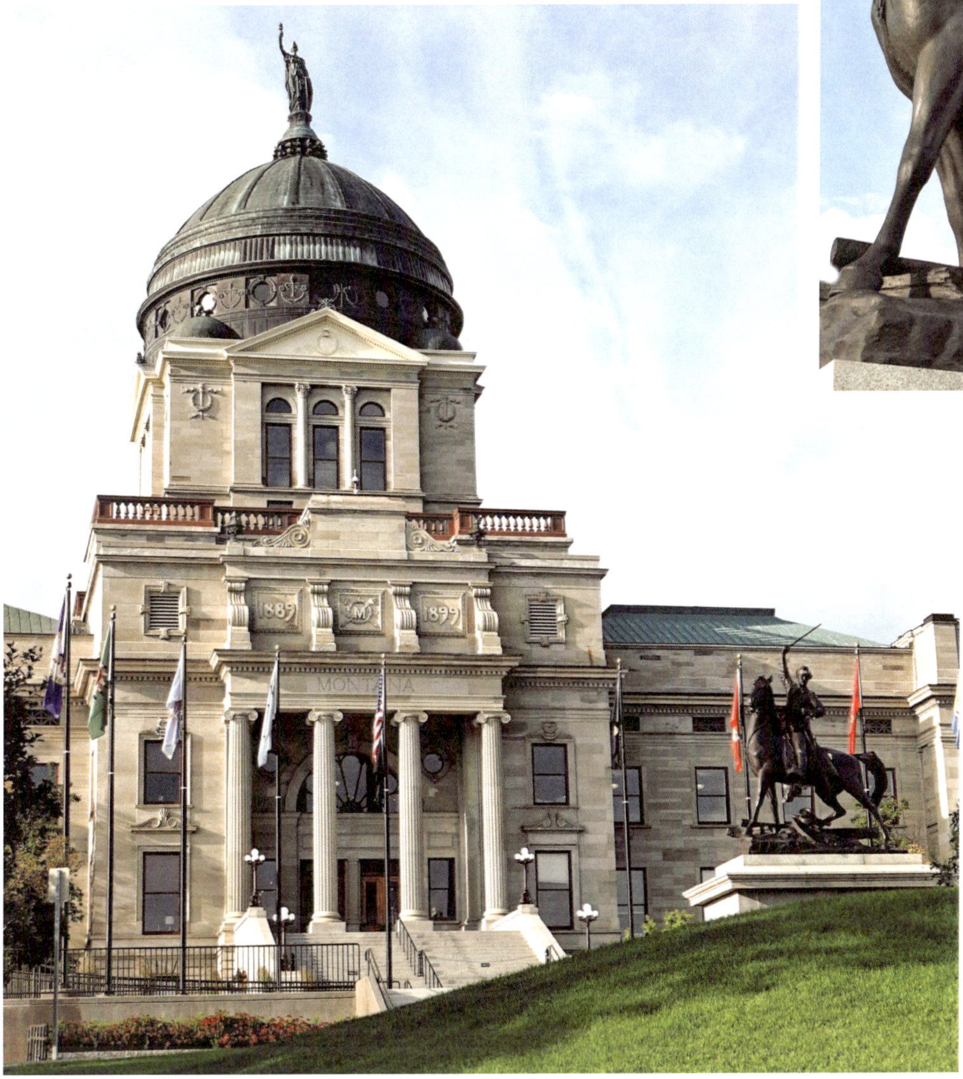

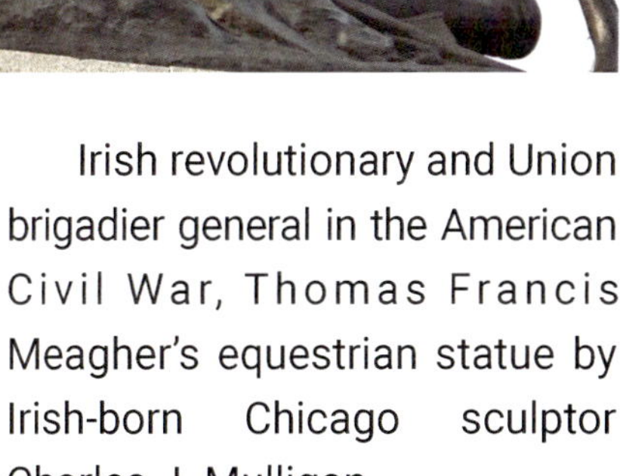

Irish revolutionary and Union brigadier general in the American Civil War, Thomas Francis Meagher's equestrian statue by Irish-born Chicago sculptor Charles J. Mulligan.

The statue is a tribute to the many Irish immigrants who made Montana their home, as it is to Meagher himself.

The Meagher Memorial Association raised $20,000 by public contributions for the statue which was dedicated on July 4, 1905.

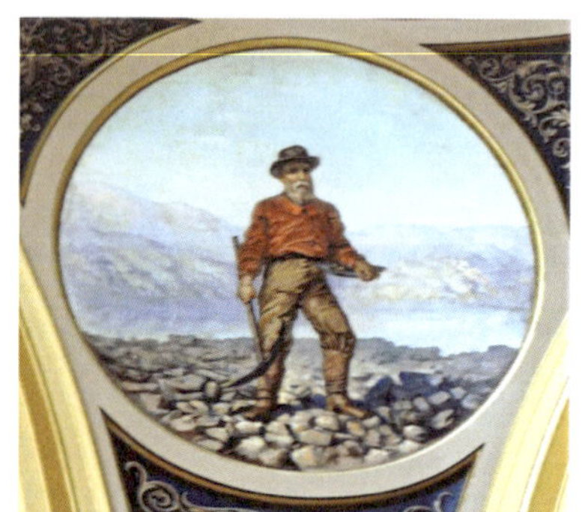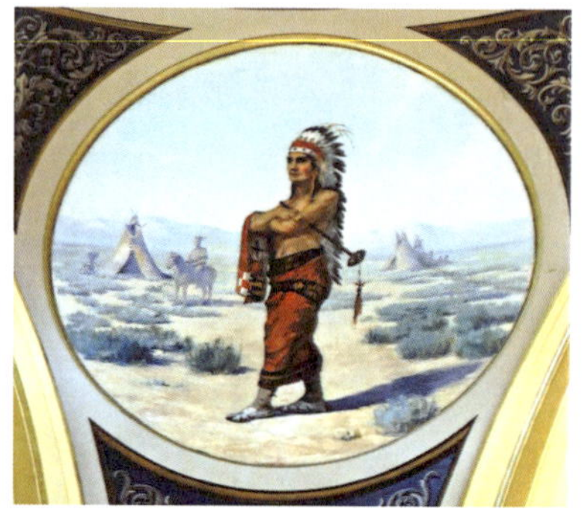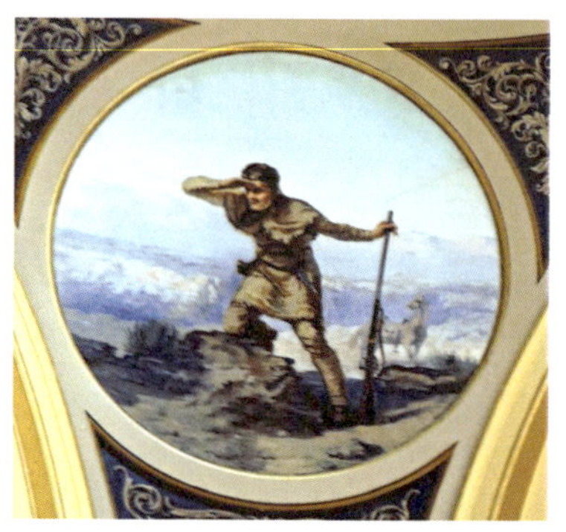

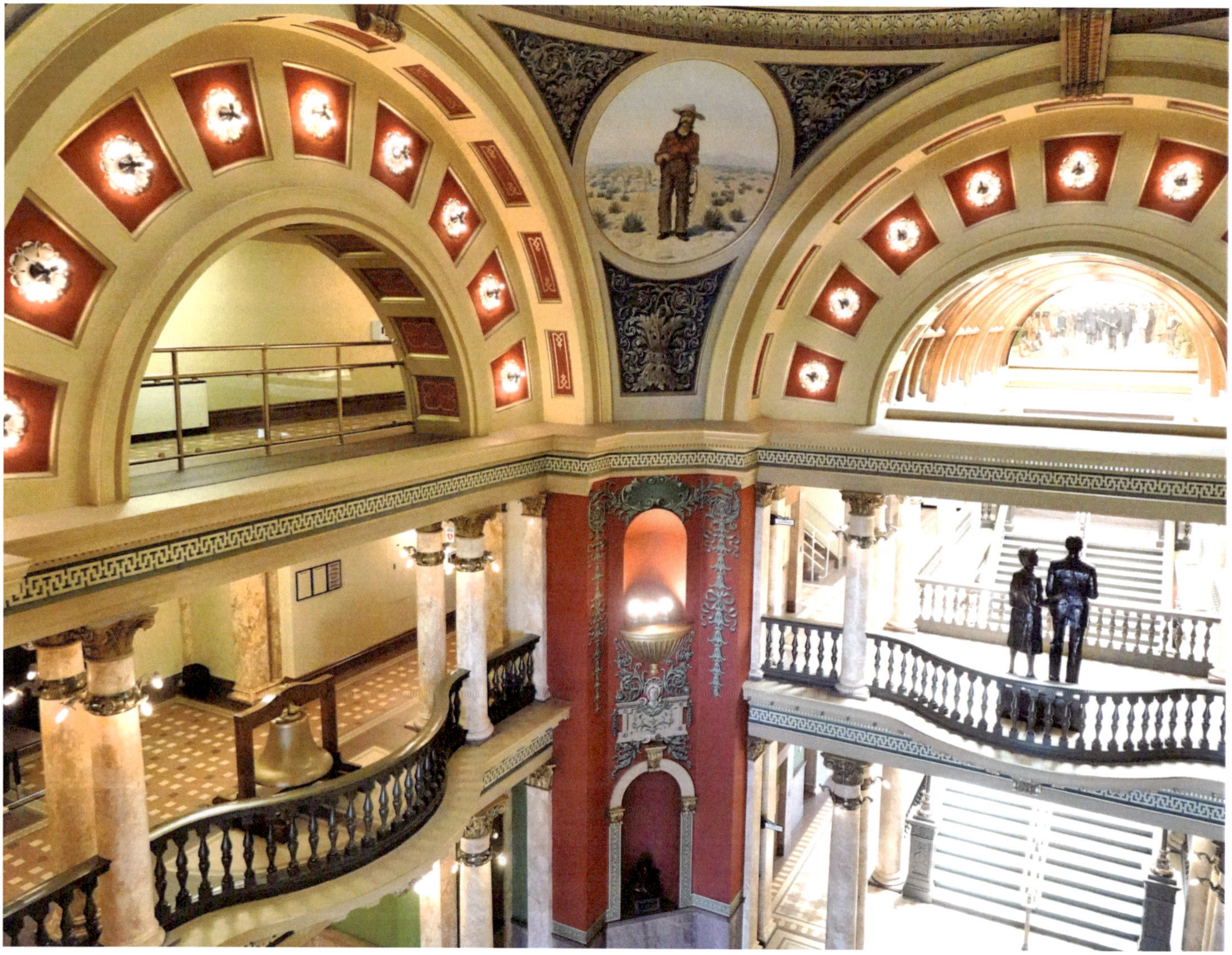

Rotunda Dome, Artwork

The rotunda at the center of the Montana capitol rises 125 feet above the second floor. F. Pedretti's sons were hired to decorate the capitol when it was built in 1899. They created many of the paintings in the building, including the four roundels in the rotunda that depict archetypes of the state's early history. *The Indian Chief* depicted Chief Charlo Salish; *The Prospector* honored Henry Finnis Edger; and *The Trapper* depicted Jim Bridger. *The Cowboy* was inspired by the artwork of Charles M. Russell and displays the typical cowboy.

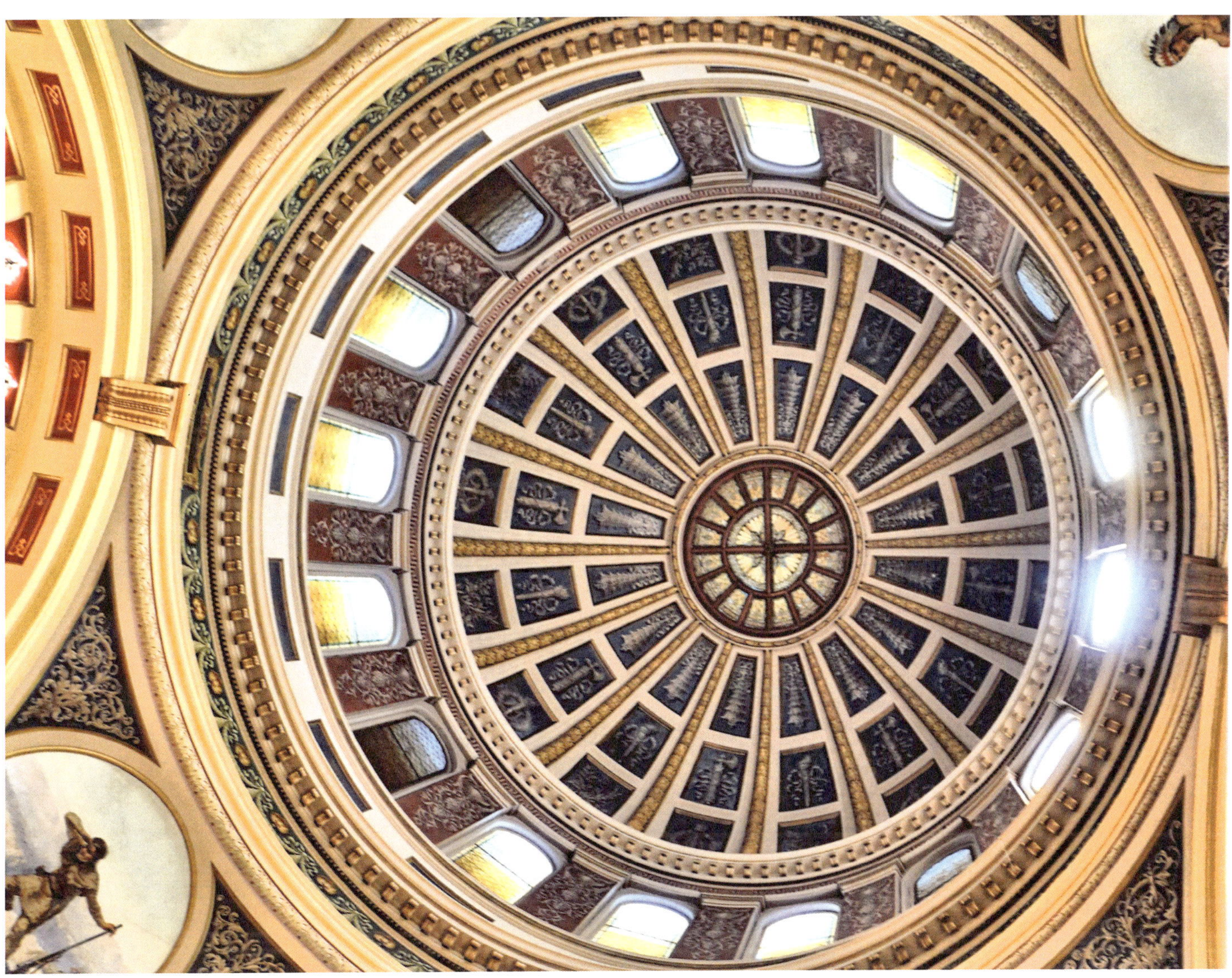

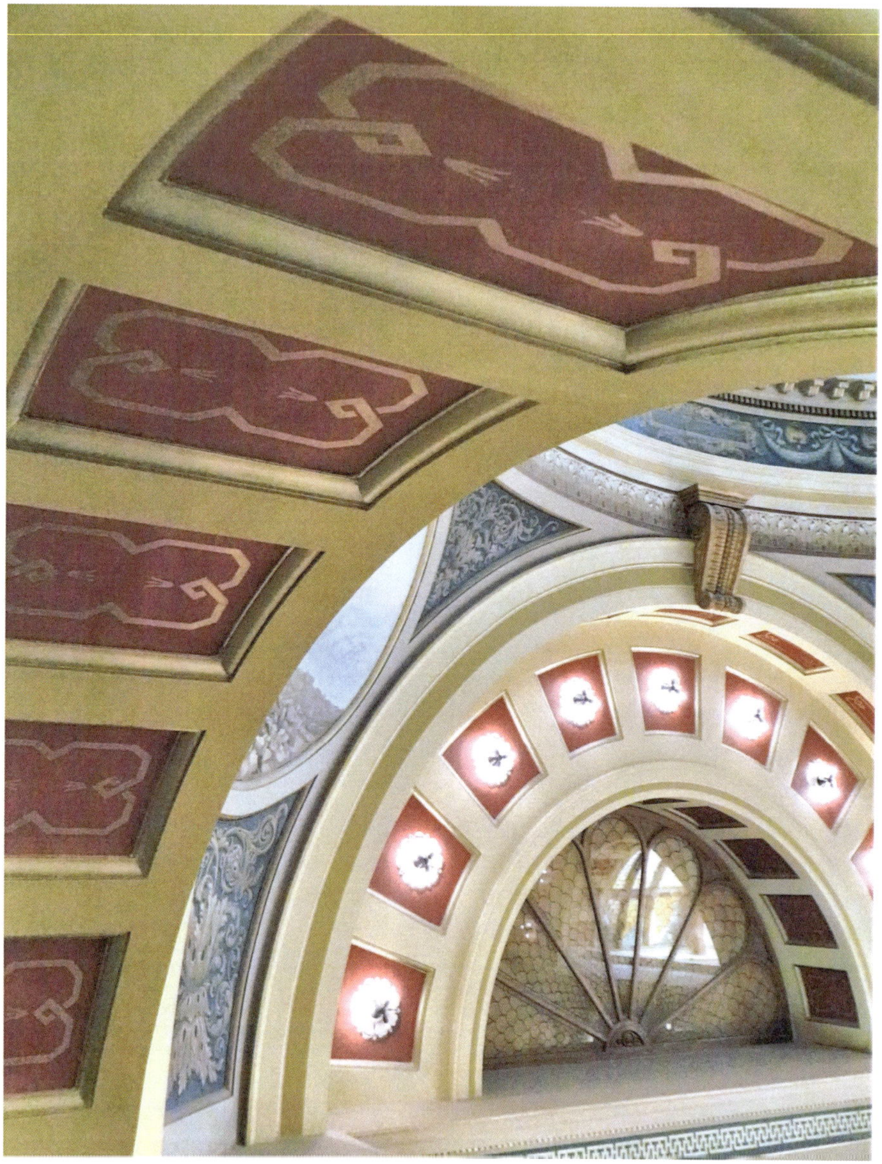

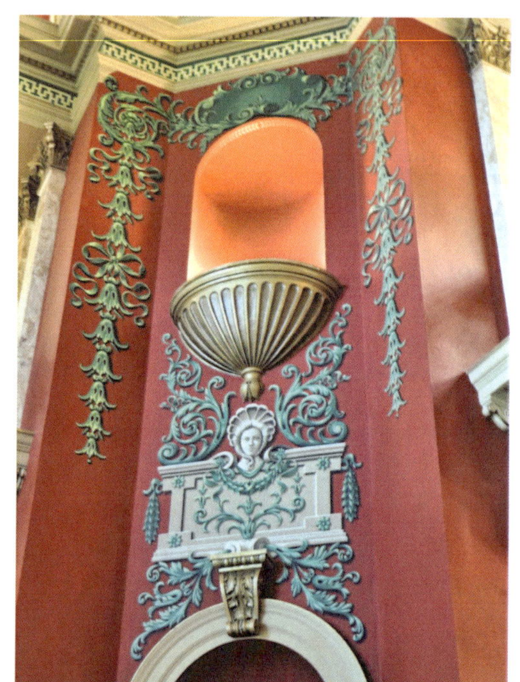

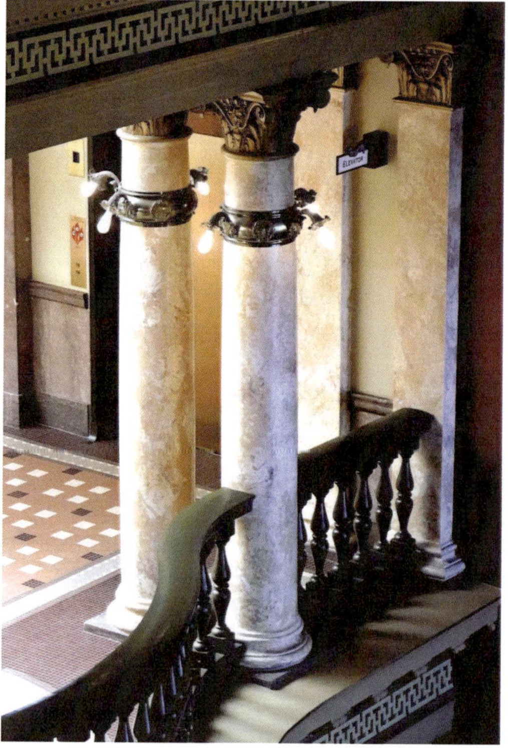

Trompe L'oeil, Scagliola

Trompe l'oeil paintings appear three-dimensional and grace the walls of the rotunda. Most of the columns in the capitol are scagliola composites of plaster with chips of marble that appear to be marble columns. The columns are hollow, allowing electrical wiring to reach the lights circling the columns.

Mansfield Statue

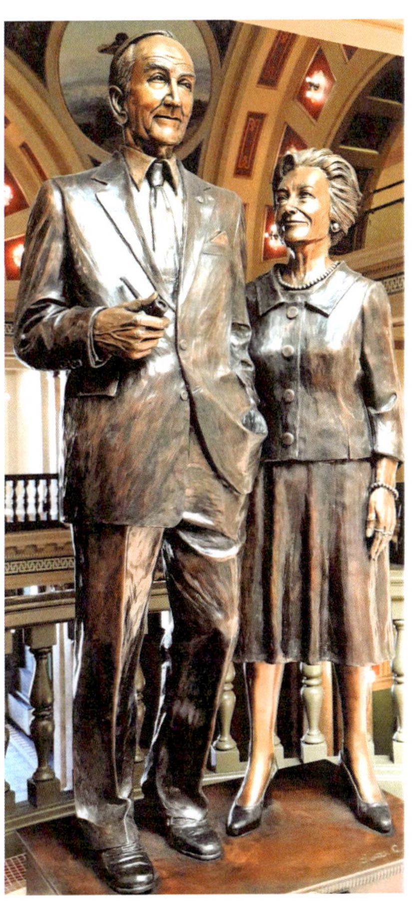

Congressman Mike Mansfield, and his wife Maureen, are honored with a statue by Gareth Curtiss created in 2001.

Mansfield was the longest serving Congressman, elected as a U.S. Representative 1942-1952 U.S. Senator 1952-1977, senate majority leader 1961-1977, and U.S. Ambassador to Japan, 1977-1989.

When the statue was created, he insisted that his wife Maureen be included, honoring the critical role she played in his career.

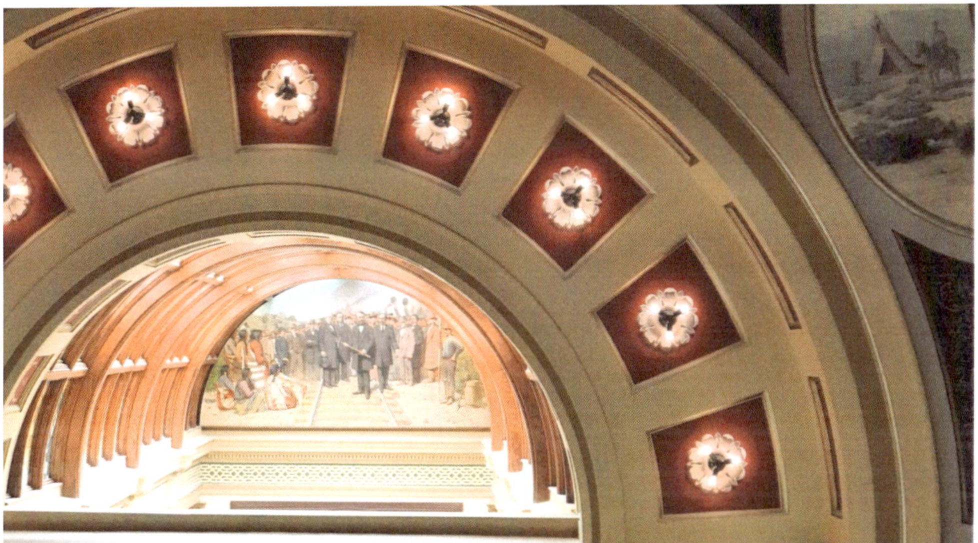

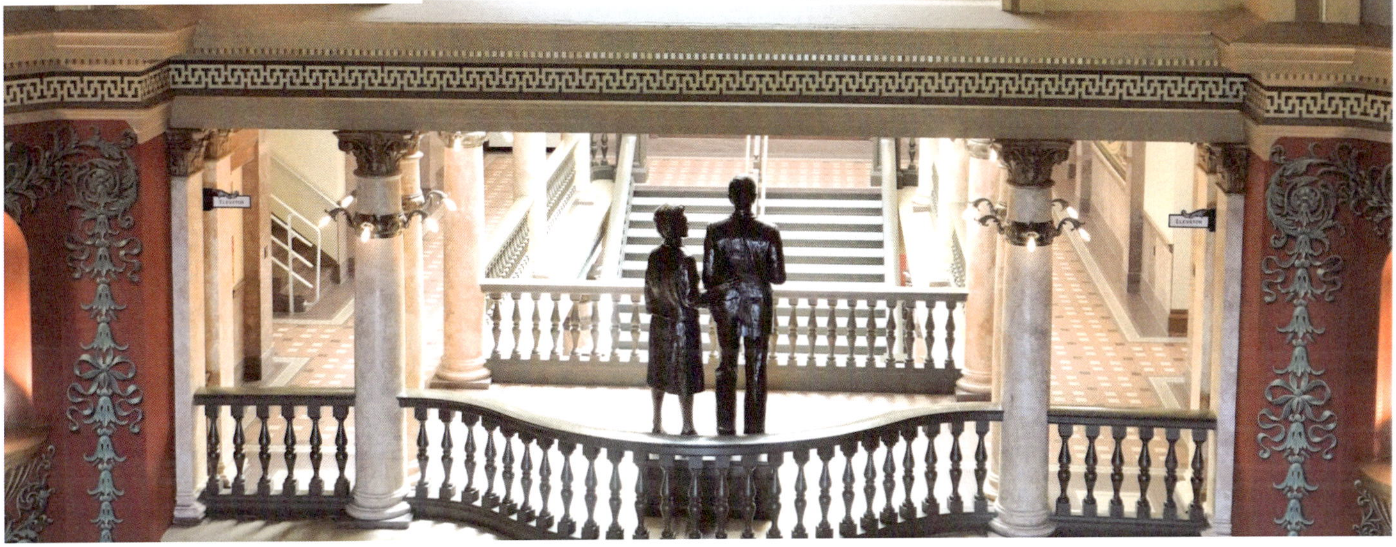

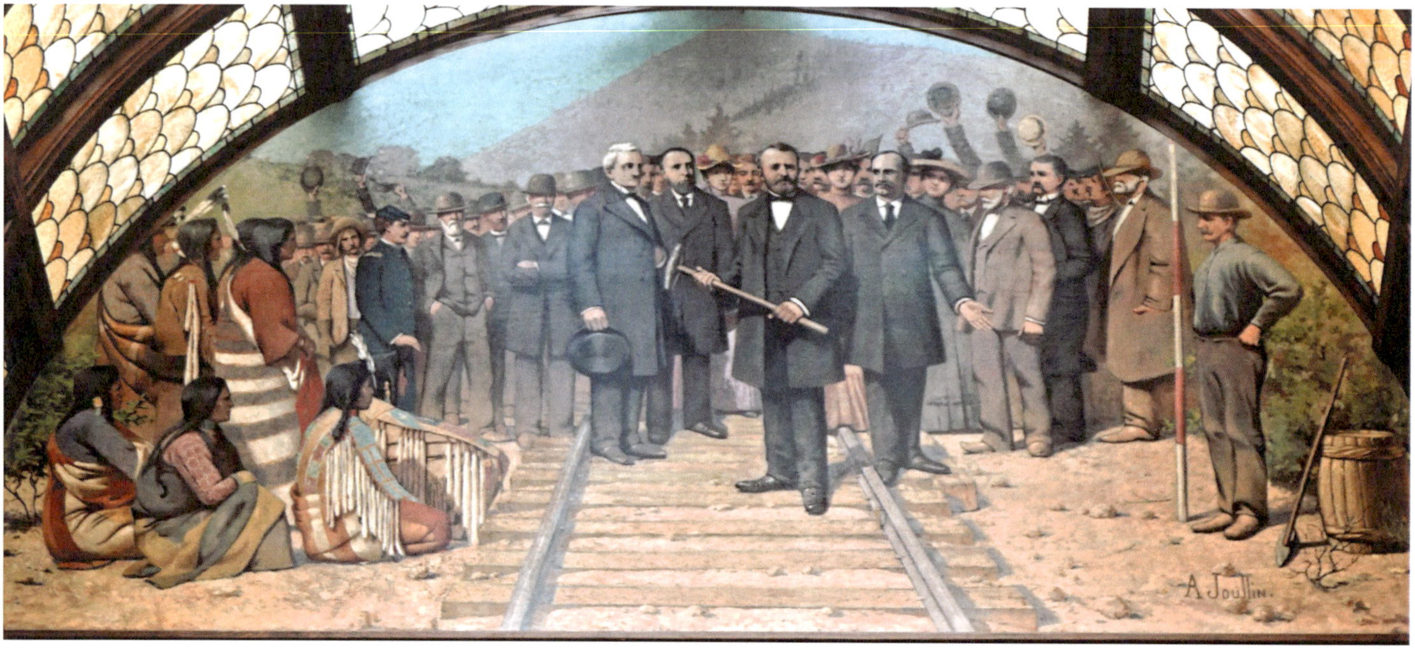

At the top of the grand staircase are two pieces of art.

The stained glass was installed in the original section of the capitol.

The mural, *Driving the Golden Spike,* depicts the completion of the Northern Pacific Railroad, Montana's first transcontinental line, in 1883.

The oil painting by Amedee Joullin was created in 1903. U.S. Grant is seen holding the sledgehammer to drive in the final spike.

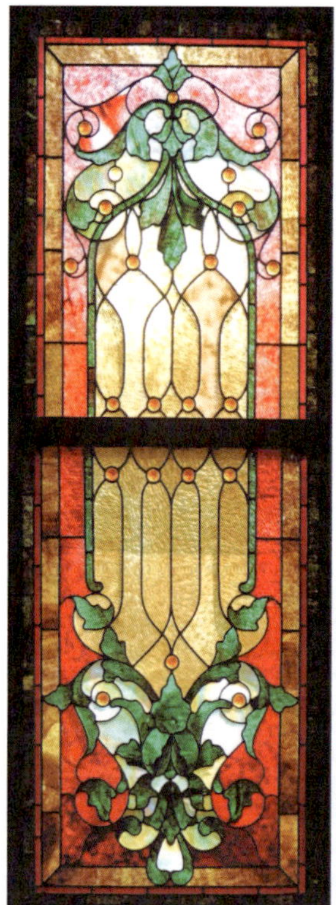

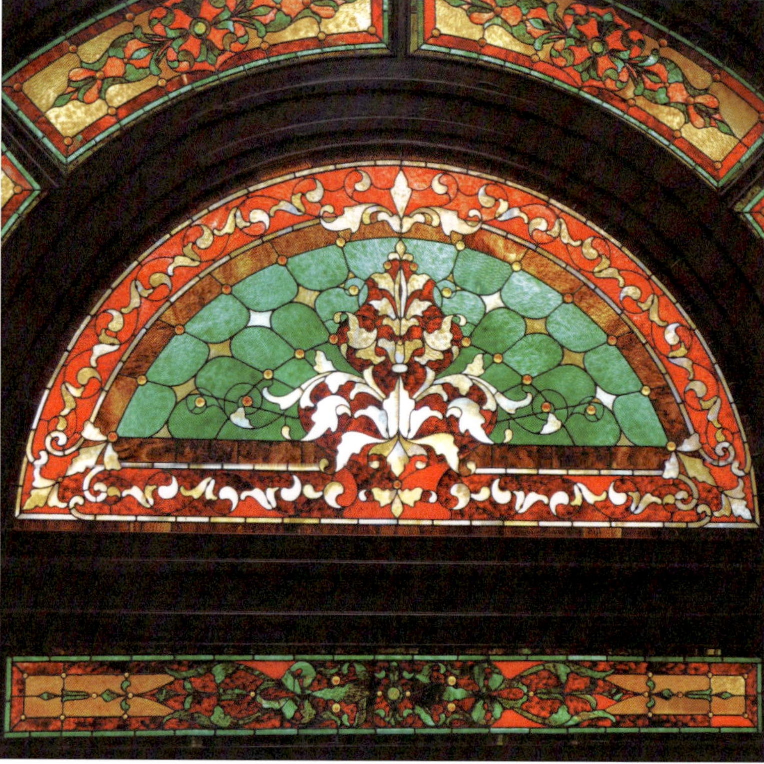

Grand Stairway

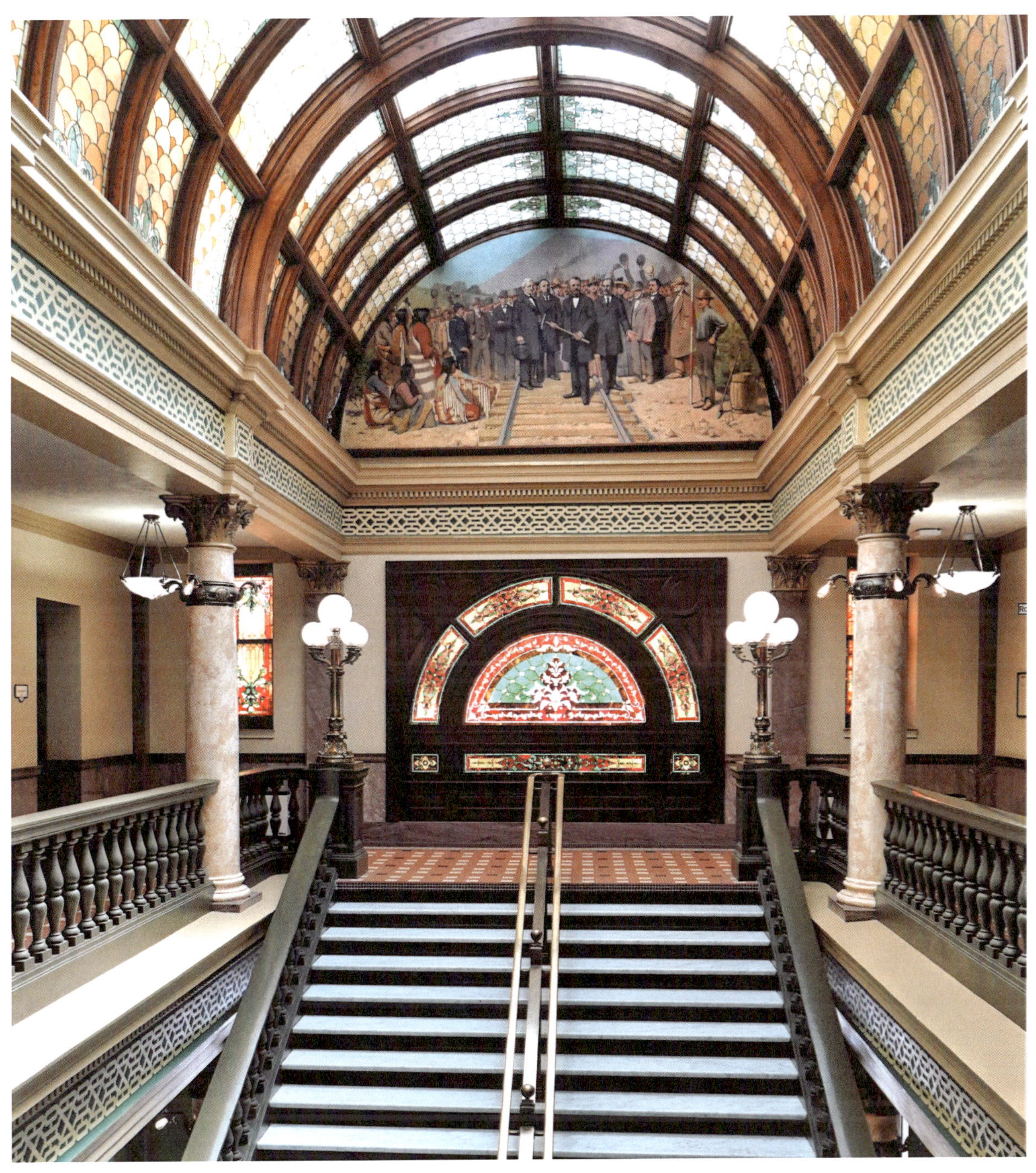

Women Build Montana Paintings

The two-part mural by Hadley Ferguson was created in 2015 after female state legislators pointed out that women were not represented in the capitol's art, yet they had contributed to the settling and cultural progress of the state.

Culture, on the east side of the staircase, and *Community*, on the westside, illustrates the essential roles played by women in Montana's story, from the traditions of Indigenous people to women's contribution to home life, politics, community building, and the workforce in the first half of the 20th Century.

Within each mural is a description of women's importance, as stated in the cutlines under each photograph

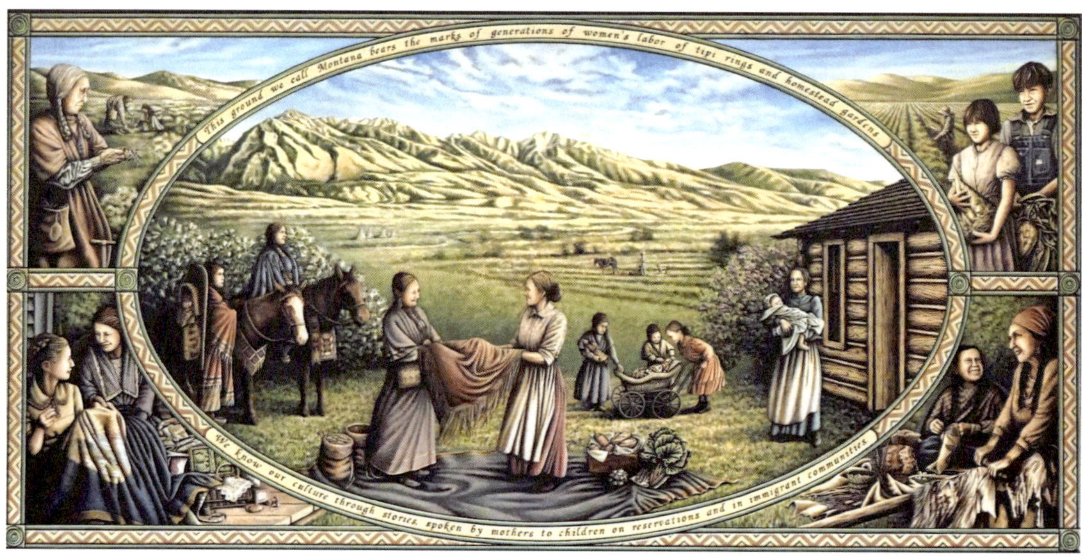

This ground we call Montana bears the marks of generations of women's labor of tipi rings and homestead gardens. We know our culture through stories, spoken by mothers to children on reservations and in immigrant communities.

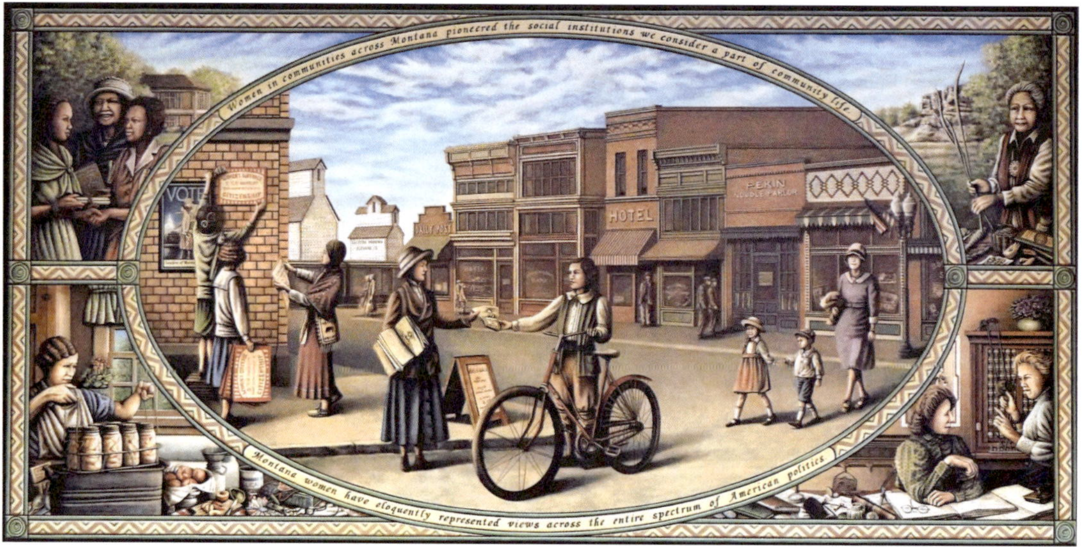

Women in communities across Montana pioneered the social institutions we consider a part of community life. Montana women have eloquently represented views across the entire spectrum of America politics.

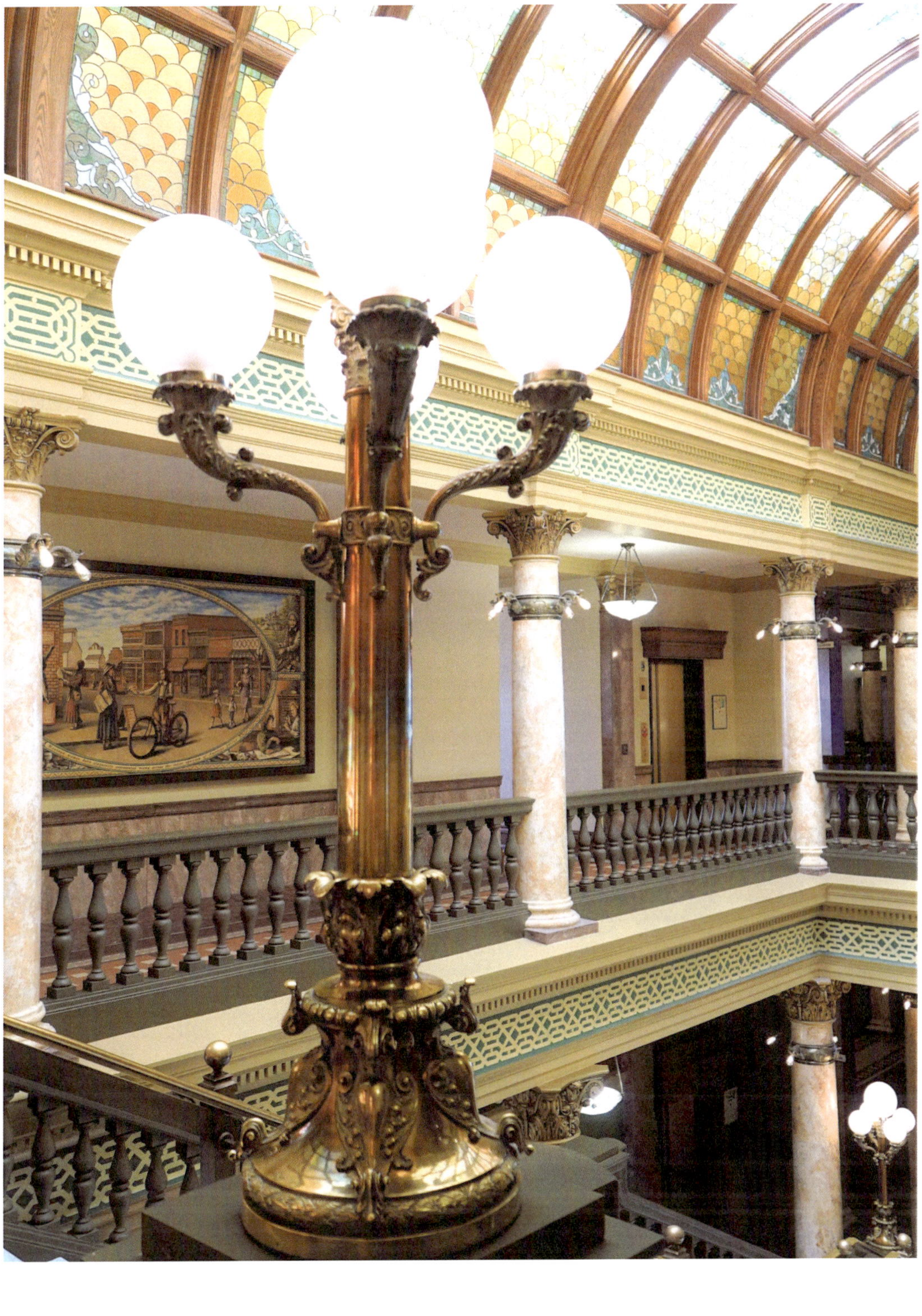

Grand Stairway Chandelier

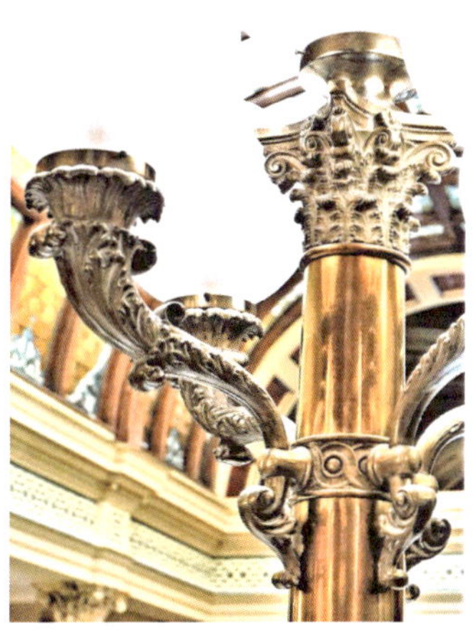

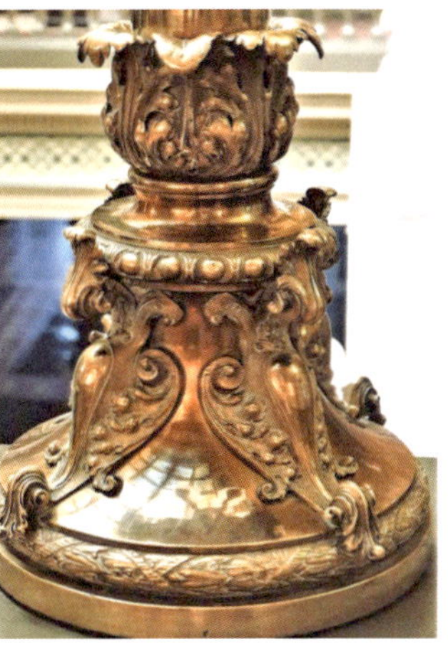

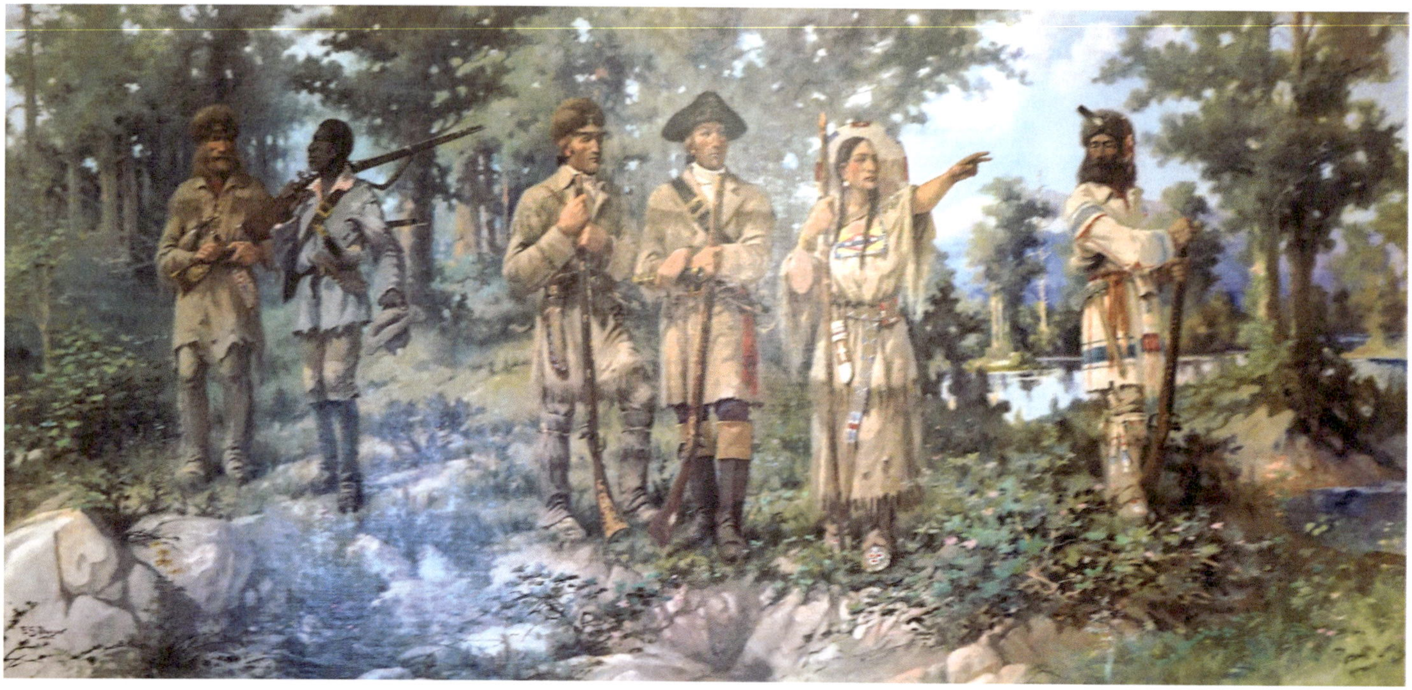

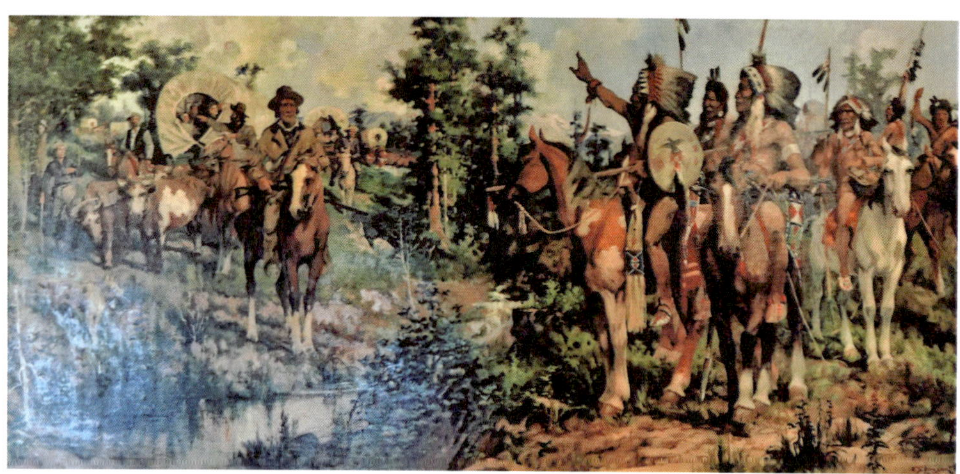

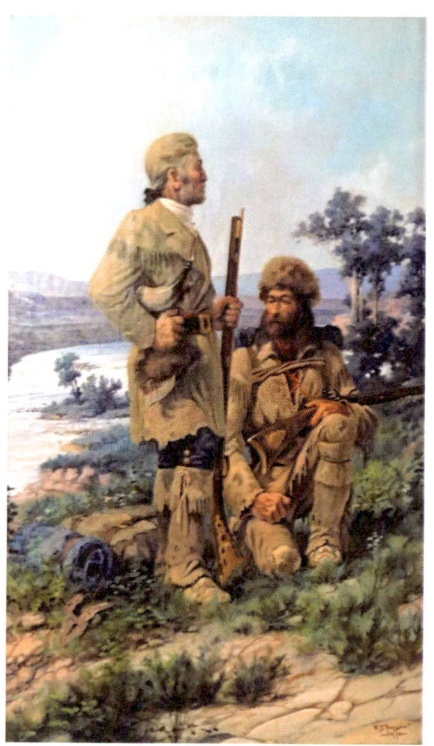

Murals in the House of Representatives lobby include *Lewis and Clark at Three Forks,* top photo; *The Border Land,* above photo; and *Meriwether Lewis at Black Eagle Falls with Jim Bridger,* right photo; as well as *After the Whiteman's Book, Pierre de La Verendrye,* and *The Surrender of Chief Joseph.*

House of Representatives Chamber

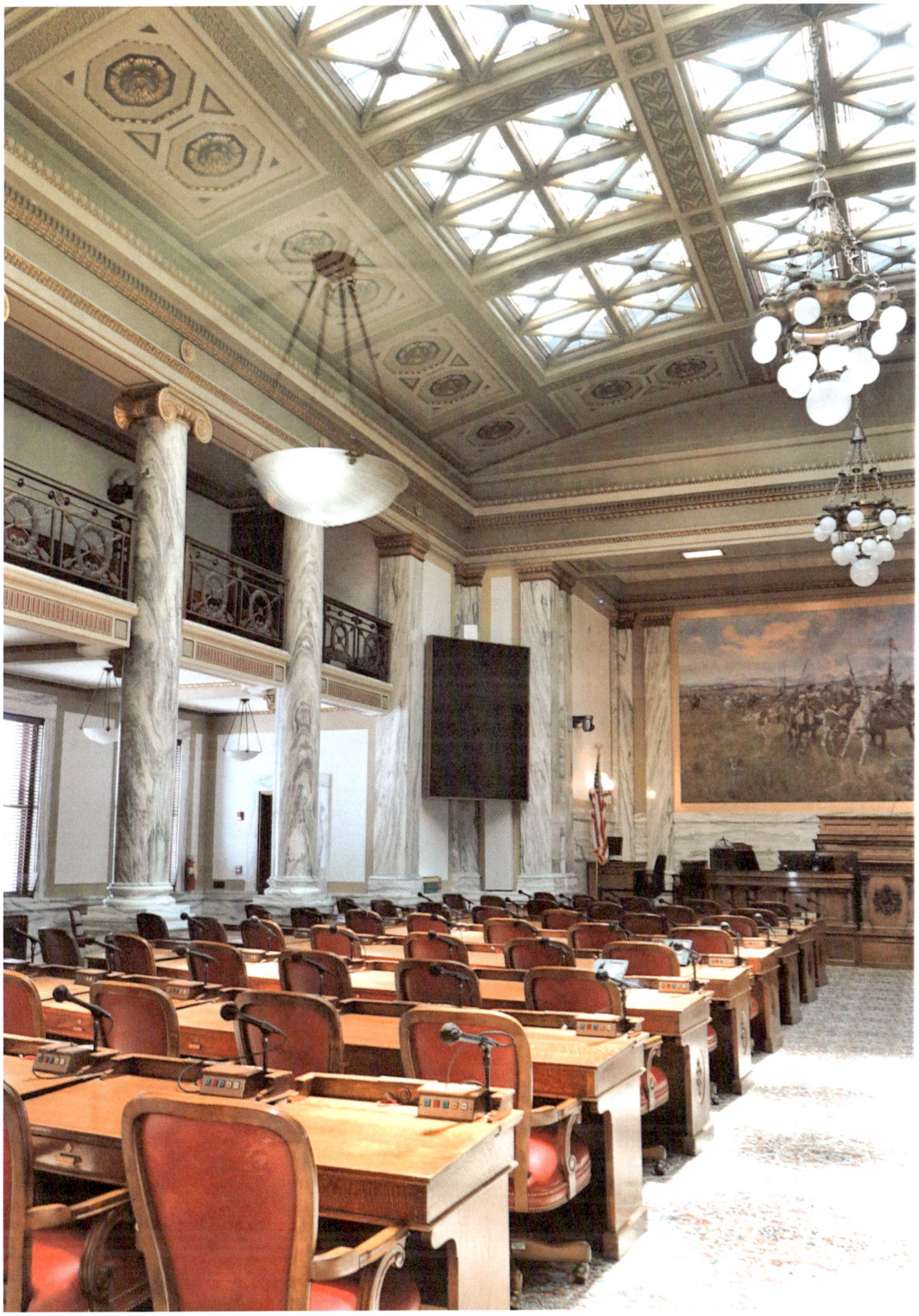

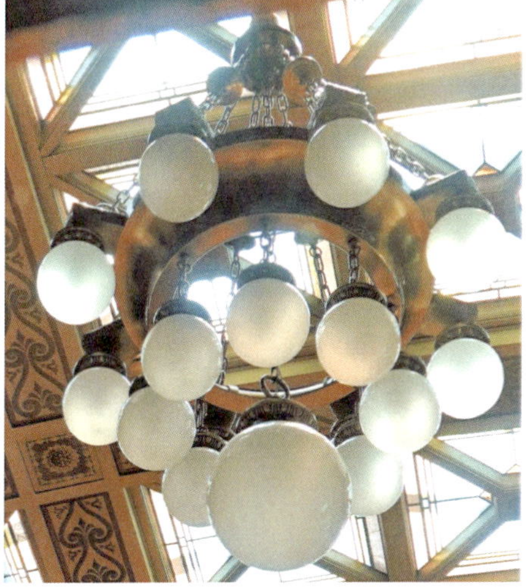

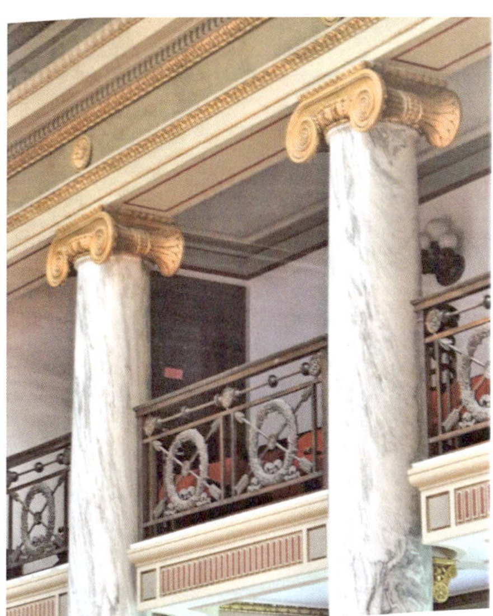

The painting behind the House of Representatives chamber's dais is Charles M. Russell's largest painting, titled *Lewis and Clark Meeting the Indians at Ross' Hole*. He painted it in 1912.

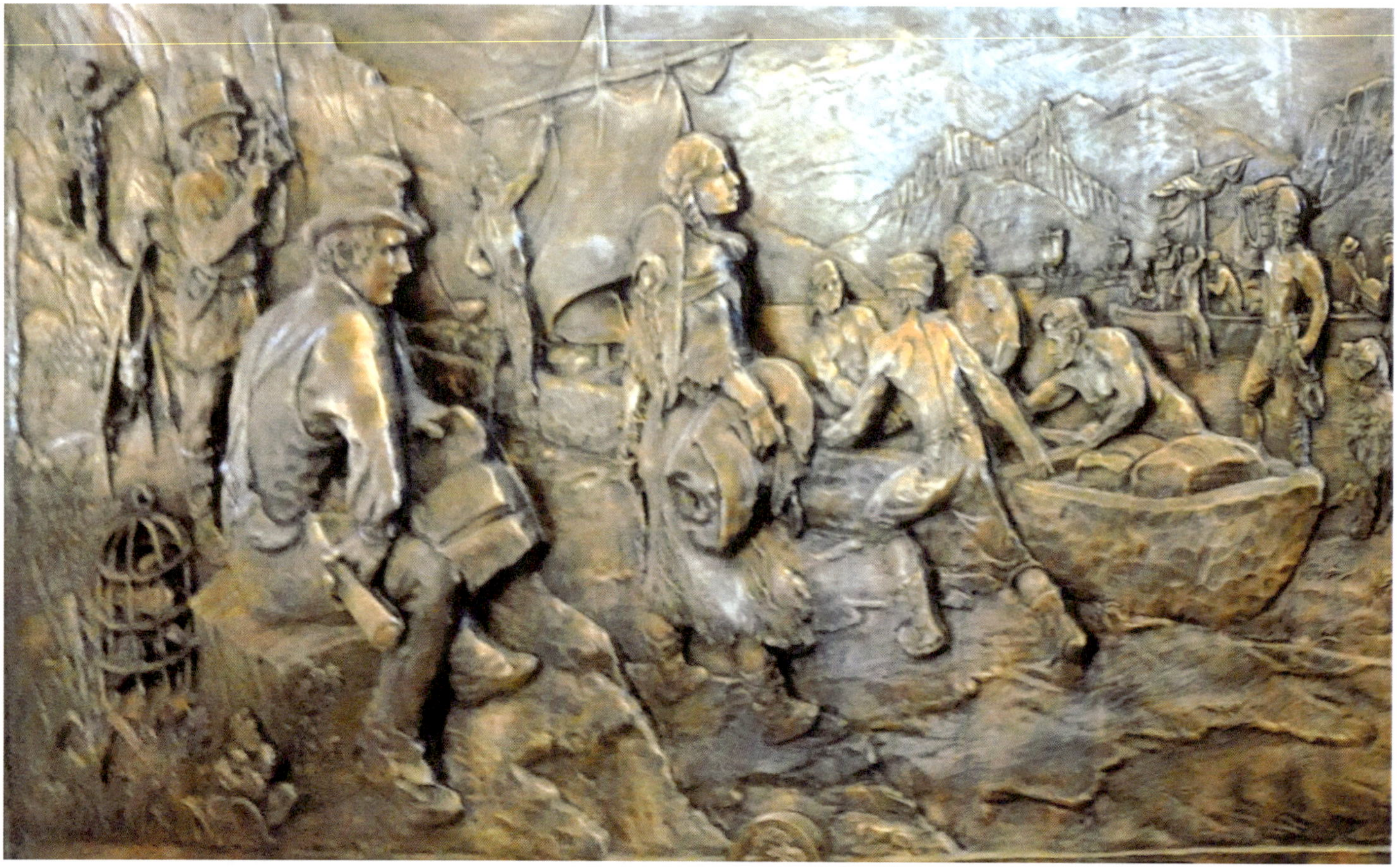

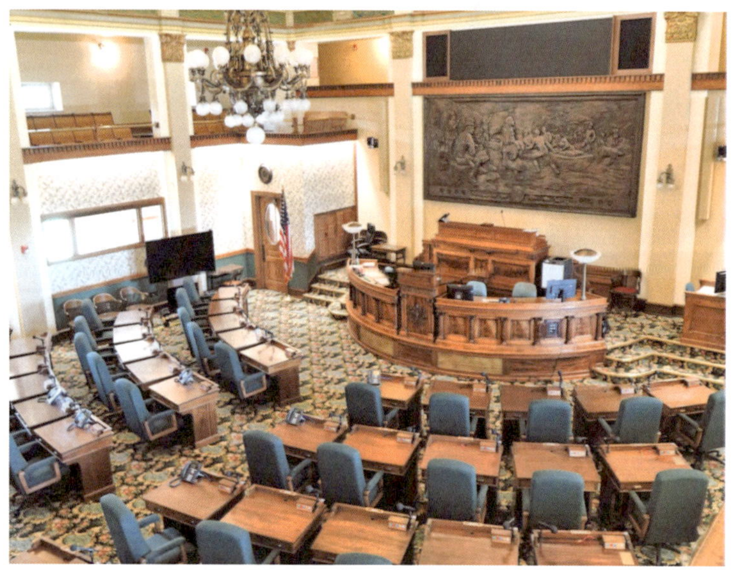

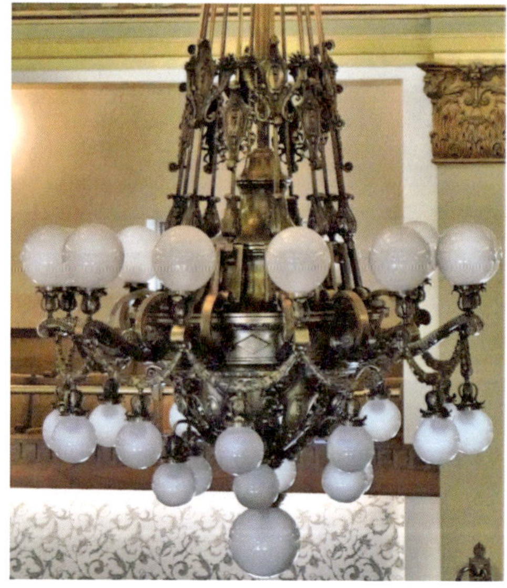

Senate Chamber

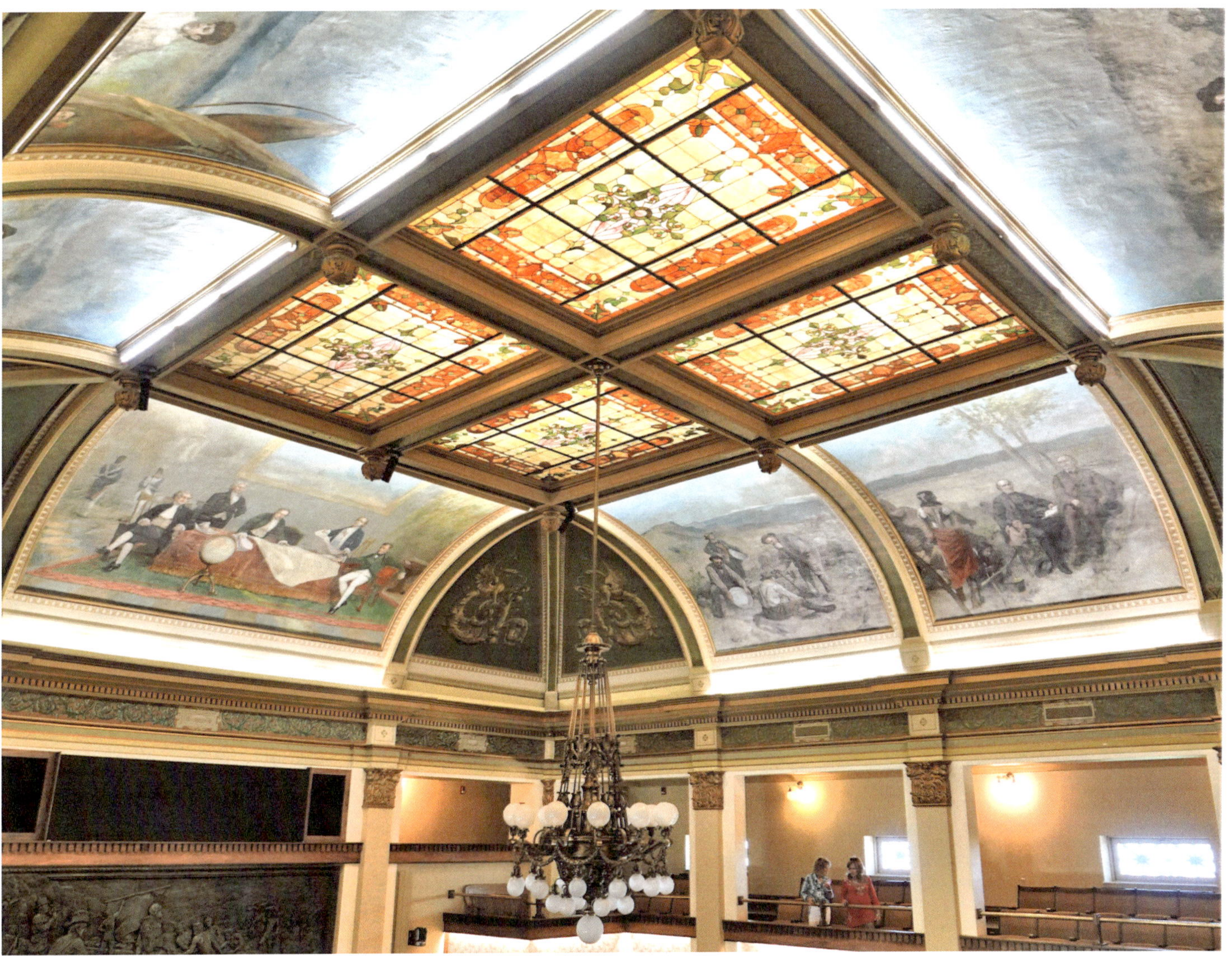

The ceiling of the Senate chamber features paintings by the Pedretti brothers that depict events in Montana history, including *The Louisiana Purchase, Prospectors at Nelson Gulch, Old Fort Owens, Custer's Last Battle, and Old Fort Benton.* At the front of the room, behind the dais, is a bronze bas-relief, We Proceeded On, by Eugene Daub, created in 2006. The bas-relief shows members of the Lewis and Clark Expedition preparing to reembark on their upriver journey. The chandelier is one of the two remaining original light fixtures. This chamber was originally used by the House of Representatives.

Murals in the Old Supreme Court include *Signing of the Enabling Act, Lewis' First Glimpse of the Rockies, Signing the Proclamation of Statehood, The Chase of the Buffalo, Farewell to the Buffalo, The Gates of the Mountains,* and *Emigrant Train Being Attacked by Indians.*

The chandelier is original to the chamber.

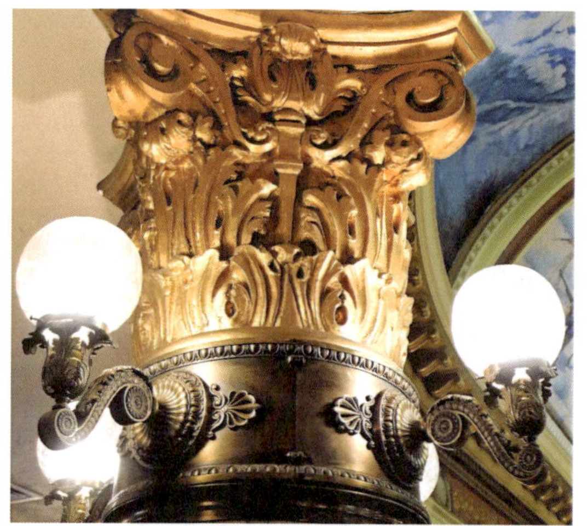

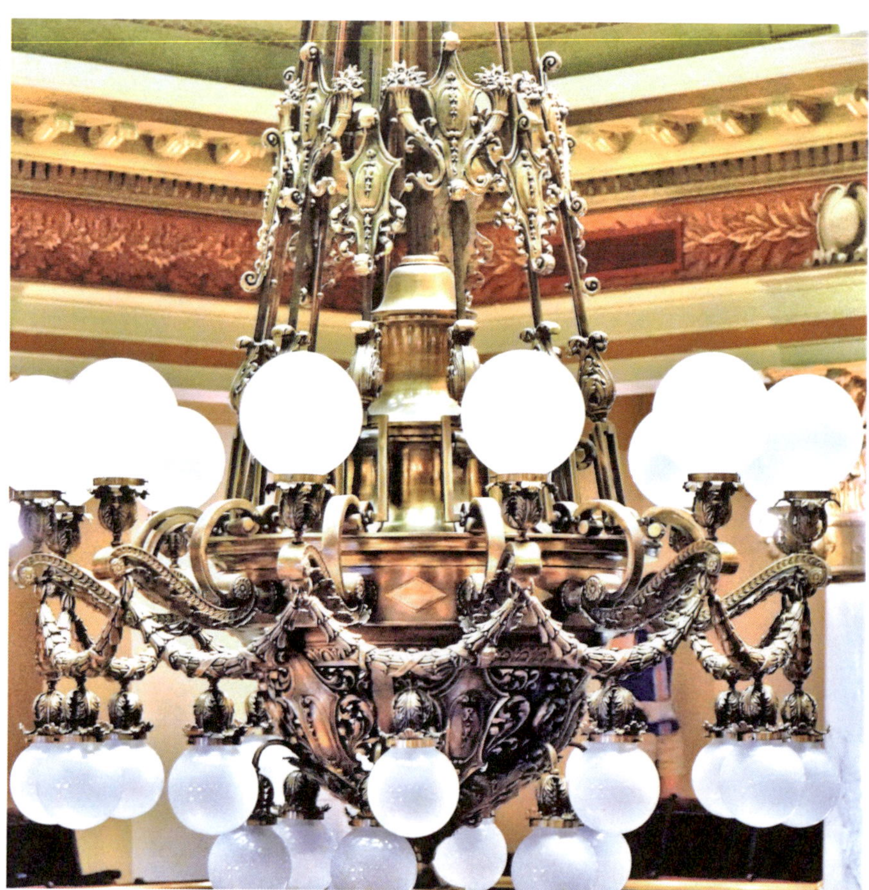

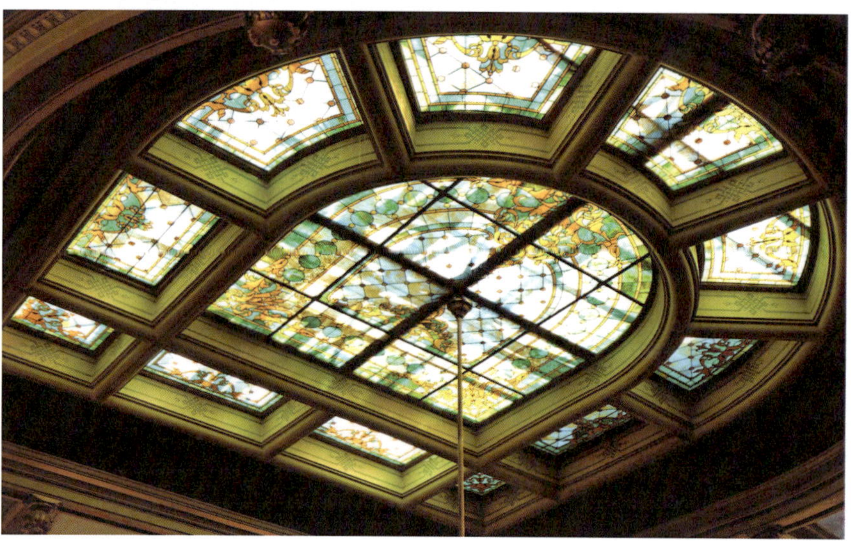

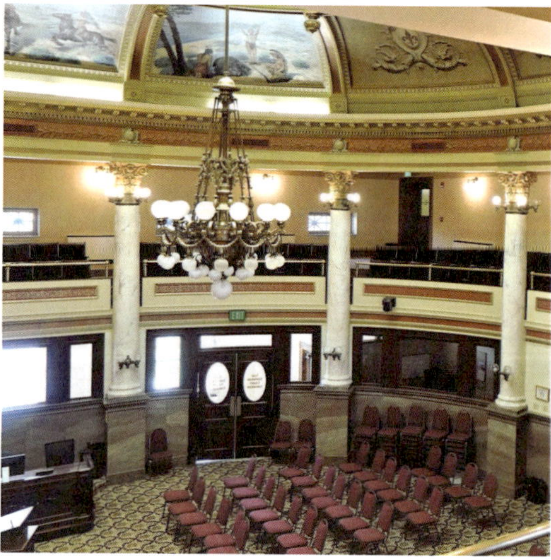

Old Supreme Court Chamber

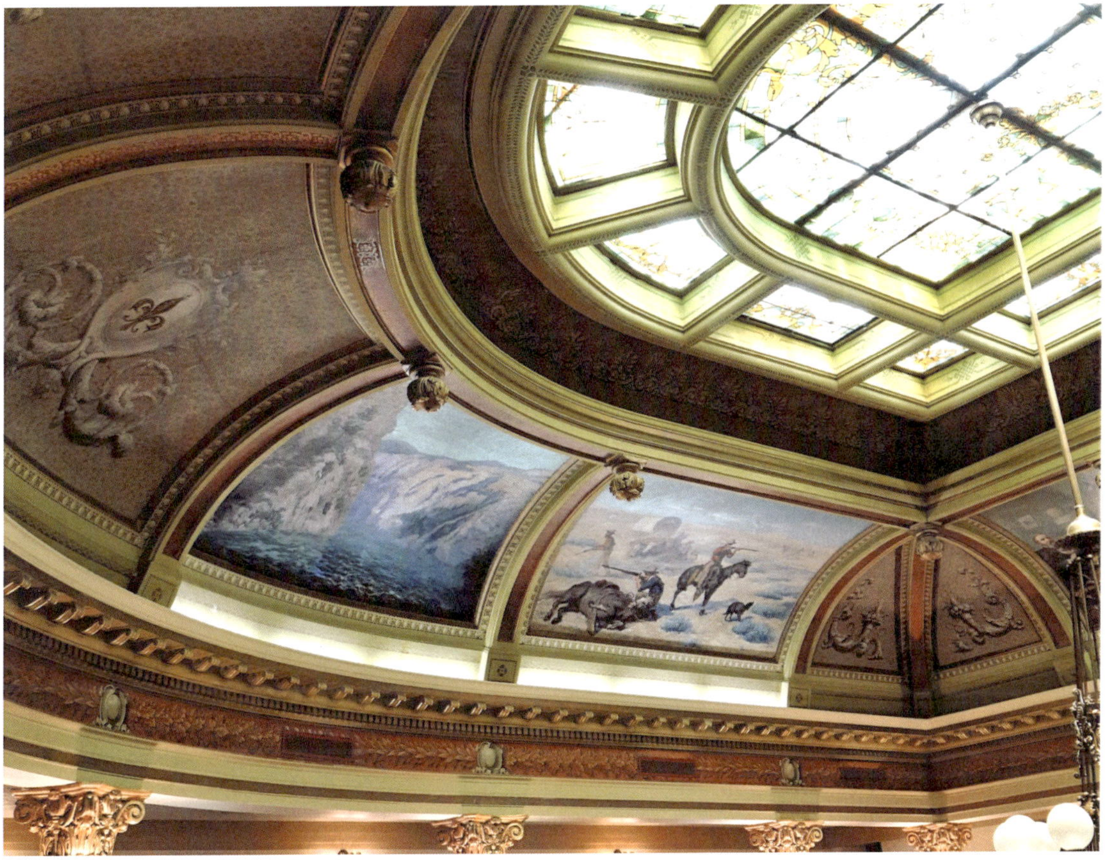

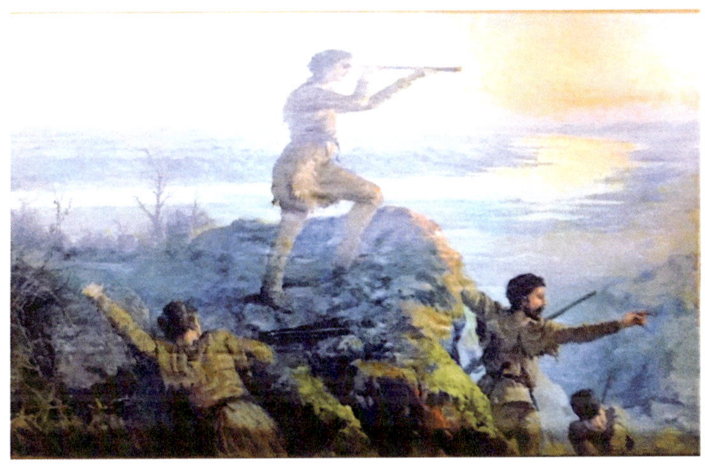

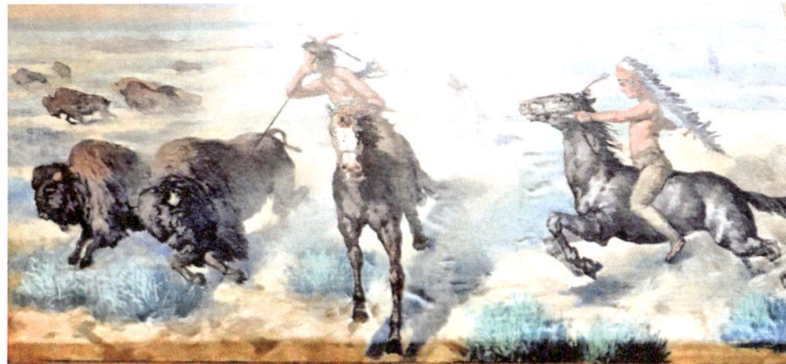

Montana State Seal

The Great Seal of the State of Montana is a vivid symbol of all that is special about Big Sky Country. It evolved from a basic design submitted by Francis McGee Thompson during the first legislative assembly of the territory in 1864.

The seal features a plow and miner's pick and shovel above the words Oro el Plata, which is Spanish for gold and silver, the two riches that gave rise to the state nickname, Treasure State.

In the background, under the big skies of Montana, are the mountains representing the Spanish origin of the state name Montana, and the Great Falls of the Missouri River which dazzled explorers Lewis and Clark.

The current seal, designed by G. R. Metten, was adopted by the third legislative assembly in 1893.

The symbolism is encircled by the words The Great Seal of The State of Montana.

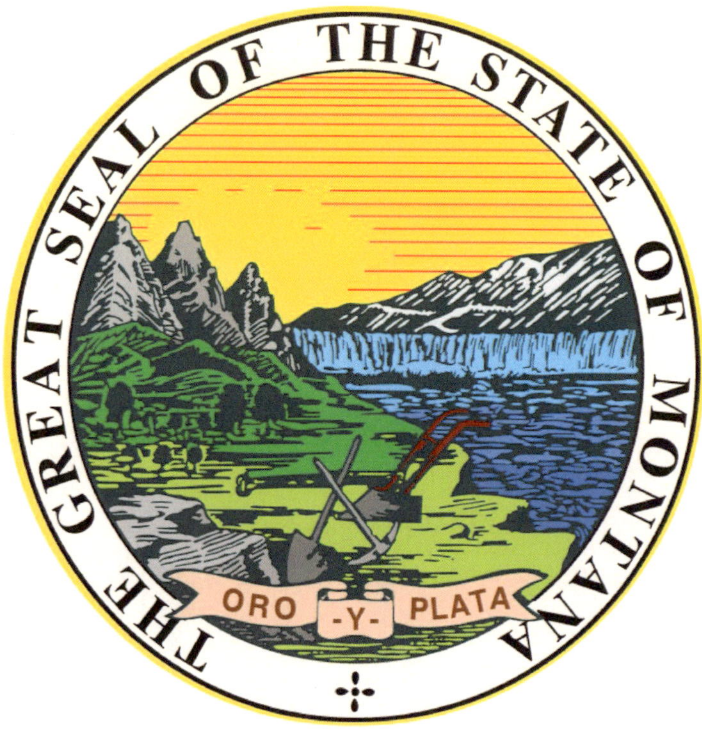

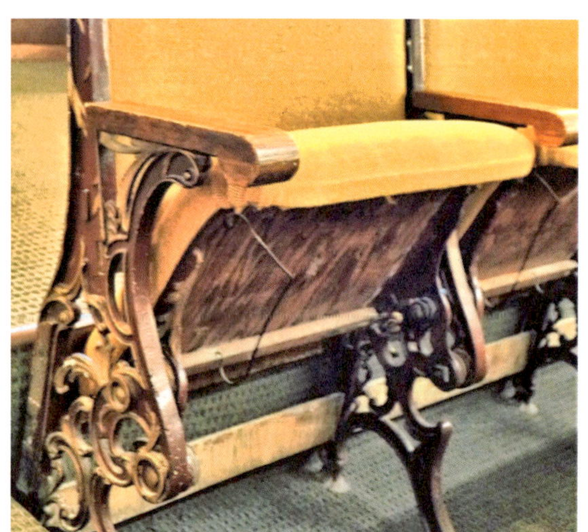

Seats with old fashion hat racks are still used in the chamber galleries.

About the Photographer

Jane Moorman describes herself as an adventurer who loves to drive the backroads to see what there is to see.

During her 30-year journalism career, Jane honed her photographic skills as a photojournalist including covering high school sporting events.

A friend once said, "I wish I could see the world as Jane sees it. Finding the beauty in things that most of us don't take time to see." Upon retiring in 2021, Jane decided there is a lot of her native country she had not visited, including each state's capitol, so she began her journey of exploring the USA.

www.ingramcontent.com/pod-product-compliance
Lightning Source LLC
Chambersburg PA
CBRC100836110726
48006CB00009B/1412